I0435650

PKSOI PAPER

Tackling Africa's First Narco-State: Guinea-Bissau in West Africa

Colonel Stephen K. Van Riper

September 2014

*****

Comments pertaining to this report are invited and should be forwarded to: Director, Peacekeeping and Stability Operations Institute, U.S. Army War College, 22 Ashburn Drive, Carlisle, PA 17013-5054.

*****

All Peacekeeping and Stability Operations Institute (PKSOI) publications are available on the PKSOI homepage for electronic dissemination.

*****

The Peacekeeping and Stability Operations Institute publishes a quarterly journal to update the peace and stability operations community on the research of our analysts, recent and forthcoming publications and upcoming conferences sponsored by PKSOI. Each quarterly journal has a specific theme related to peace and stability operations and a commentary by the Director of PKSOI entitled *The Director's Corner*. If you are interested in receiving this journal, please subscribe on our homepage at *http://pksoi.army.mil/subscription.cfm*.

*****

DEDICATION

Dedicated with sincere thanks to Karen Finken-binder, Larry Bouchat, and LtCol Chris Watkins (USMC, Ret). The encouragement, mentorship, and great information provided by all throughout this project is greatly appreciated.

Special acknowledgement to Nissa Van Riper for her inspiring and inexhaustible patience in editing and improving this complex work.

FOREWORD

The United Nations coined the term 'transnational crime' in the 1970s to call attention to criminal acts which transcended national jurisdictions, such as money laundering, terrorist activities, illicit arms trafficking, illicit drug trafficking, trafficking in persons, and corruption. These types of activities inherently undermine progress in the peace and stability operations environment and deter foreign assistance in affected areas.

The author explores how Guinea Bissau contributes to regional and global instability. The U.S. identified Guinea Bissau as Africa's first narco-state due to its prominent position along known transnational crime smuggling routes. The author advocates U.S. involvement with Guinea Bissau or risk losing influence in West Africa. Van Riper also provides recommendations building upon existing cultural values to strengthen the state and rid itself of the affliction of drug smuggling. "Tackling corruption, neutralizing spoilers, and increasing the societies' culture of lawfulness are necessary steps to save West Africa."

It is our pleasure to bring to you this monograph.

Daniel A. Pinnell
Colonel, U.S. Army
Director, PKSOI

ABSTRACT

The U.S., Europe and regional African players must tackle drug smuggling in West Africa to prevent that region from falling into chaos. Today, West Africa is a significant nexus for the illegal trafficking of oil, weapons, cigarettes, drugs and other commodities. The United States has labeled Guinea-Bissau Africa's first narco-state and it has become the epicenter of a region where Transnational Criminal Organizations are corrupting governments and societies at an alarming rate. Their nefarious efforts, and Guinea-Bissau's state failure, conflict with U.S. stated interests. Tackling corruption, neutralizing spoilers, and increasing the societies' culture of lawfulness are necessary steps to save West Africa. This will be challenging in Guinea-Bissau due to geography, culture, government structure, and a corrupted military. But with the right adjustments to resources, authorities and priorities, it can be done.

ABOUT THE AUTHOR

Colonel Stephen K. Van Riper was born in Fort Bragg, North Carolina. He received a Bachelor of Arts in History at the University of Florida in 1993, a Masters in Adult Education from Kansas State Uni¬versity in 2005, a Masters in Operational Art from the US Marine Corp's School of Advanced Warfare in 2006, and a Masters in Strategic Studies from the US Army War College in 2014.

He was commissioned in May 1993 and, after completing the Infantry Officers Course, reported to 3rd Battalion, 7th Marines where he served as a Platoon Commander, and then as the Weapons Company Executive Officer. He participated in a Joint Task Force - 6 Counter Drug Operation in California and Operation United Shield in Mogadishu, Somalia. In August of 1997 he was promoted to Captain and transferred to teach at The Basic School. Captain Van Riper served as a Staff Platoon Commander and Executive Officer. He taught Patrolling, Tactical Planning, and Military Operations other than War. In 2000 he attended the Amphibious Warfare School. He graduated in 2001 and took command of Weapons Company, 3/1. As the Commanding Officer he deployed on a six month deployment aboard ship and then as part of Operation Iraqi Freedom I. Upon return from Iraq, he became the Director of 1st Marine Division Schools.

In 2004-2005 Major Van Riper attended the U.S. Army Command and General Staff Officers Course in Ft Leavenworth, KS and then the U.S. Marine Corps' School of Advanced Warfighting in Quantico, VA. From 2006 - 2009, he served as a served as a Future Operations Planner for the I Marine Expeditionary Force and then Regimental Combat Team 1. This tour saw him deploy to Iraq twice. His experiences in Iraq led him, in 2009, to become the Chief Instructor and then the Operations Officer for the Marine Corps Operations and Tactics Group.

In the summer of 2011, LtCol Van Riper moved to St. Louis Missouri to serve with 3rd Battalion, 24th Marines. As the Battalion Inspector-Instructor he mentored the reserve leadership and commanded the active duty component. In August 2013, LtCol Van Riper transferred to Carlisle, PA where attended the US Army War College. In 2014 he was assigned to US Central Command and is presently serving as the Strategy and Policy Officer within the CCJ-5.

Col Van Riper's decorations include the Meritorious Service Medal with three stars, the Navy and Marine Corps Commendation Medal with star, the Navy and Marine Corps Achievement Medal, the Combat Action Ribbon with star, and a Sea-Service Deployment Ribbon with five stars.

Col Van Riper is married to the former Nissa Weaver of Dowagiac, Michigan. They have one daughter, Ellis who is 6.

Tackling Africa's First Narco-State: Guinea-Bissau in West Africa

Introduction

In 2013, the United States labeled Guinea-Bissau as Africa's first narco-state.[1] If regional trends continue, it will not be the last West African nation to bear that moniker. Due to an unfortunate mix of location, culture, and history, West Africa is a growing hub within the international drug markets. Today, Guinea-Bissau is the center of that hub and its situation is worsening by the day. While such a small country in the massive continent of Africa would not usually warrant much interest from the United States, it cannot be ignored that Guinea-Bissau's fate may determine if West Africa rises or falls. Considering President Obama stated in 2012 that "Africa is more important than ever to the security and prosperity of the international community, and to the United States in particular,"[2] allowing Guinea-Bissau and West Africa to slide into chaos is counter to U.S. strategic interests. This paper will briefly describe the overall regional issues, focus on Guinea-Bissau's issues, discuss challenges to any counter-drug campaign and then recommend a way ahead for dealing with Guinea-Bissau -- the tip of the West African drug iceberg. In the end, this paper hopes to prove that the way ahead in preserving U.S. interests in West Africa revolves around rebalancing Guinea-Bissau's government's structure while also making drugs a taboo smuggling commodity.

World Wide Drug Issue

Illicit drugs are between a $150 billion and $500 billion dollar business annually.[3] By some accounts it is two percent of worldwide GDP and, despite significant effort by nations and international bodies, shows no sign of declining.[4] As a global enterprise it contains all of the elements of any successful market -- robust production networks, flexible and adaptive transportation systems, strong distribution arrangements, and stout financial systems to move funds and protect assets.[5] Market demand is high and those involved in the business are doing well.

> The UNODC [United Nations Office for Drugs and Crime] has suggested that seizure levels would need to be consistently 75% of total production in order to inflict sustained damage on the traffickers' business model. Optimistically, annual seizures are reported as amounting to 40% of total populations. But since we have only the haziest idea of the quantities of illegal narcotics produced or consumed in the world, or what the value of this trade amounts to, it is impossible to know how much is truly taken out of circulation[6].

This success has caused international drug trafficking organizations (DTOs) to expand their portfolios and delve into other illicit activities such as arms smuggling, human trafficking, terrorism, money laundering, and insurgency. As DTOs have morphed with other illicit organizations the United States has begun to label them as Transnational Criminal Organizations (TCO).[7]

> Transnational organized criminals act conspiratorially in their criminal activities and possess certain characteristics which may include, but are not limited to:

- In at least part of their activities they commit violence or other acts which are likely to intimidate, or make actual or implicit threats to do so;

- They exploit differences between countries to further their objectives, enriching their organization, expanding its power, and/or avoiding detection/apprehension;

- They attempt to gain influence in government, politics, and commerce through corrupt as well as legitimate means;

- They have economic gain as their primary goal, not only from patently illegal activities but also from investment in legitimate businesses; and

- They attempt to insulate both their leadership and membership from detection, sanction, and/or prosecution through their organizational structure.[8]

But TCOs are not simply DTOs which have expanded. Drug profits have also been sought by insurgents looking to expand their war chests, arms dealers looking to capitalize on their trafficking routes with other high-value commodities, human traffickers "selling" couriers, and criminal gangs seeking more businesses to "protect."

Due to their transnational nature, TCOs have focused on four categories of drug that have high worldwide demand, sufficient supply, and significant profit. Marijuana, while lucrative and prevalent, does not have nearly the profit margin of the other three: synthetics (including meth and ecstasy), heroin and cocaine.[9] These last two, especially cocaine, are contributing extensively to the problems in West Africa and will be the focus of the remainder of this paper.

Cocaine production is focused in South America. "Because of the geographic idiosyncrasies of growing the coca plant, crops are limited to the Andes region of South America, specifically in the countries of Bolivia, Peru and Colombia, and along the border areas of Ecuador and Venezuela."[10] Colombia produces about 54 percent of the refined cocaine on the world market, with the rest coming from Bolivia and Peru.[11] "[T]he cocaine exporting business is relatively young. Although coca and cocaine were commercially available in Western societies before its prohibition, its illicit trafficking skyrocketed in the 1970s and fully matured in the 1980s."[12] Most of this maturation impacted the United States. But in the early 2000s, things began to change.

West Africa's Regional Drug Issue

As the world entered the 21st century, cartels in South America saw a shift in world cocaine markets. The United States market became saturated while the European market began to expand dramatically. According to the UN International Narcotics Control Bureau, the cocaine market doubled and tripled in parts of Western Europe beginning in 2000[13]. The cartels responded by establishing new routes to meet the increased need. "West Africa, which neither produces nor consumes significant quantities of cocaine, [became a] victim to changes in global supply and demand."[14]

West Africa was ideally positioned geographically, politically, economically, and culturally to become a major transit point as TCOs shifted eastward.[15] Located almost equidistant from major ports and airfields in South America and Europe, West Africa became a significant stopping point for aircraft and ships making the journey. With challenged governments and large swaths of ungoverned spaces, the cartels found ample room to establish bases with little risk of interference and almost no threat of arrest or prosecution.[16] As a region with the majority of its citizens living at the bottom of the world's economic ladder, there were plenty of people looking to earn a living. And with hundreds of year's worth of smuggling as part of their heritage, the West African culture was conducive to aiding the South American drug cartels in establishing routes, bypassing border controls, and moving products quickly and effectively. [17]

> Drug planes don't have to fly below the radar, because in most cases there is no radar (or electricity). Soldiers sometimes help smugglers by closing airports and unloading the cargo. Police cars run out of gas when giving chase or are left in the dust by smugglers' all-terrain vehicles. There are no local navies to intercept ships coming from Latin America or to chase 2,000-horsepower boats that speed drugs up the coast to Europe. Traffickers are seldom brought to trial; in some cases, there are no prisons to put them in. Even when they are charged they are usually released because evidence is not collected or needed laws are not in place.[18]

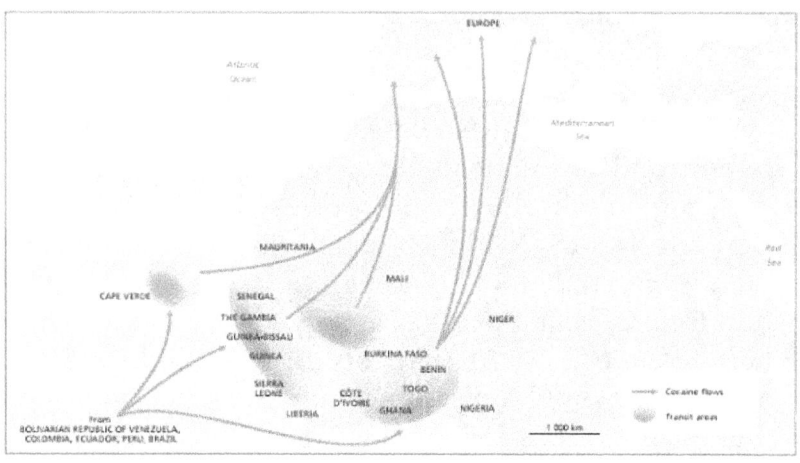

Figure 1. Drug Trafficking Routes in West Africa

By 2004, West Africans were providing significant assistance to cocaine traffickers[20] and by 2007 "estimates of annual cocaine transshipments in West Africa range[d] between 60 and 250 tons, yielding wholesale revenues of $3 billion to $14 billion."[21] "By some measures, 50 percent of non-U.S.-bound cocaine now goes through West Africa, i.e., about 13 percent of global flows."[22] Approx 80% percent of the traffic arrives by sea in as many as one hundred ships, while the other 20% percent travels by illicit aircraft landing all across West Africa.[23]

As this traffic arrives it often finds ample labor due to West Africa's significant economic straits. It also finds governments unable to impede cocaine traffic flow, or willing to support the traffickers in return for financial rewards.[24] "West Africa is now facing a situation analogous to the Caribbean in the 1980s, where small, developing, vulnerable countries along major drug-trafficking routes toward rich consumers are vastly under-resourced to deal with the wave of dirty money coming their way."[25] It is well on its way with multiple Latin American DTOs already maintaining bases in over two-thirds of West African nations.[26]

Why This Matters to the United States

At this point it seems prudent to discuss why what appears to be a primarily European and African problem is of interest to the United States. U.S. interests lie along two fronts: combating TCOs and embracing Africa. President Obama in his *Strategy to Combat Transnational Crime* stated:

> In the National Security Strategy [of 2010], I committed my Administration to the pursuit of four enduring national interests: security, prosperity, respect for universal values, and the shaping of an international order that can meet the challenges of the 21st century. The expanding size, scope, and influence of transnational organized crime and its impact on U.S. and international security and governance represent one of the most significant of those challenges.[27]

> [Transnational organized crime] threatens U.S. interests by taking advantage of failed states or contested spaces; forging alliances with corrupt foreign government officials and some foreign intelligence services; destabilizing political, financial, and security institutions in fragile states; undermining competition in world strategic markets; using cyber technologies and other methods to perpetrate sophisticated frauds; creating the potential for the transfer of weapons of mass destruction (WMD) to terrorists; and expanding narco-trafficking and human and weapons smuggling networks.[28]

> Transnational organized crime (TOC) poses a **significant and growing threat** to national and international security, with dire implications for public safety, pub-

lic health, democratic institutions, and economic stability across the globe.[29] [Bolding by Author]

This "significant and growing threat" collides with our rising interest in an "Africa [that] is more important than ever to the security and prosperity of the international community, and to the United States in particular."[30]   In the *U.S. Strategy toward Sub-Saharan Africa*, the President lays out three efforts that will be critical to the future of Africa: strengthening democratic institutions, boosting broad-based economic growth, and prioritizing efforts to empower the next generation of African leadership.[31]   Since TCOs seek to weaken democratic institutions, undermine legitimate economic growth, and co-opt leaders at all levels to make profit and expand markets, their interests and ours collide in a region of the world that is at a significant tipping point -- toward order or toward chaos. Currently, the TCOs are winning and the area is tilting toward chaos. David E. Brown, an African focused Foreign Service Officer and former member of AFRICOM stated, in the governance arena "Cocaine trafficking is becoming integral to how West Africa is governed. Political actors are using criminal organization as an aspect of statecraft, and criminal actors are using political privileges as business assets."[32] In the economic arena, "illicit drug trafficking in West Africa—by far the most lucrative transnational criminal activity—has become institutionalized and so entrenched that it is essentially a part of each country's economy, making a huge, though unofficial, contribution to national income."[33] To make matters worse, the "illicit profits earned by Latin American drug cartels operating in West Africa strengthen the same criminal elements that traffic drugs to North America, and the same North African and Middle Eastern terrorist groups and nations that target the United States."[34] And lastly, in the developing tomorrow's leaders arena, "narcotics trafficking is also fraying West Africa's traditional social fabric and creating a public health crisis, with hundreds of thousands of new drug addicts."[35] Tomorrow's African leaders will have more issues to deal with, a more fractured society with which to combat issues, and a population significantly hooked on some of the world's most destructive drugs. Today these problems are most evident in a small coastal nation that few people have ever heard of.

Guinea-Bissau's Issues

Guinea-Bissau's troubles began when Portugal colonized it in the 1500s. Surrounded by countries colonized by the French it became isolated. With an official language of Portuguese, and a currency different from its neighbors, Portuguese Guinea's regional connections eroded.[36] Over time, it became politically cut off within West Africa and extremely reliant on Portugal. Unfortunately, Portugal was not interested in developing its colony, only in exploiting it. Over five centuries Portugal failed to build a strong local government or even to unite the tribes into a state with any real national identity.

In 1950, an independence movement began with the formation of the *Partido Africano da Independência da Guiné e Cabo Verde* (PAIGC). In 1963 PAIGC turned the movement violent and after eleven years of fighting, Portuguese Guinea gained its independence in 1973. The new government promptly changed the country's name to 'The Republic of Guinea-Bissau' and put in place three mechanisms that kept the new government disjointed and corrupt.

First, instead of rebuilding connections with its African neighbors and the various tribes within its borders, the government remained tied to its Portuguese sponsor and other Portuguese speaking countries. It has largely remained so to this day, being more connected to its eight Community of Portuguese Language Countries (CPLP)[37] brethren than to its fifteen *Economic Community of West African States* (*ECOWAS*) partners. Instead of finding new sponsors to assist its feeble economy, or to build a strong set of institutions, it kept its lusophone political identity and relied on Portuguese-speaking states as it struggled to become a new nation. By doing so it failed to escape the grasp of political spheres more apt to exploit resources than to represent populations.

Second, it lionized its military. Having gained its independence because of the valiant fight of its armed forces, the government honored them. As Christopher Clapham, a renowned author on African international affairs stated, liberation leaders often have a "deep sense of conviction in the…entitlement and responsibility of the survivors to continue to exercise the power."[38]

> This mentality became deeply engrained within Bissau-Guinean society, particularly among leading military officers. It contributed to a growing sense of military entitlement to shape the country and its politics. Written in 1984 and last revised in 1996, the constitution's treatment of the military is emblematic of this perception. The document not only addresses the military as an institution within the state's architecture, but also it singles out certain members of the military who deserve special perquisites and accolades above and beyond those allotted to the military as a whole.[39]

The military leadership took on a king-maker role that led to multiple coups, a federal budget skewed toward the military, and elite within the country who are largely untouchable. "No elected president has ever completed a term in office. All but one have been deposed by the military, including a coup d'état in the midst of national elections in April 2012."[40] This is possible because the defense sector accounts for 30 percent of the government budget, providing military leaders enormous influence. They have used that influence to shape the military[41] and the government to the liking of the military elite.[42] "The expanding politicization of the armed forces has upended Guinea-Bissau's weak [political] system of institutional checks and balances as well as the more formidable but unofficial balance of power among different groupings of influential elites."[43]

Third, it built a governmental system that is 'winner-take-all.'[44] Guinea-Bissau's government is a democratic republic where the President holds a majority of the legitimate power, but where the military holds ultimate power. During its 40 years as an independent state there has been a constant struggle between the Parliament, the President and the military elite. Historically the President trumps the Head of Parliament at every encounter, and the military deposes the President whenever he grows powerful enough to challenge it. This political system prevents the development of strong checks and balances. Subsequently, corruption is endemic.

Compounding Guinea-Bissau's political issues is the fact that the nation is extremely poor. The roots of the country's economic difficulties originate far in the past. Portugal, the colonial power until 1973–74, was itself relatively undeveloped, and until a very late stage was never willing or able to develop its colony. Instead, it opted for the maintenance of traditional economic structures with a view to ensuring political control, alongside the extraction of mercantile profits from a small number of crops like groundnuts and cotton.[45]

According to the World Bank, today (40 years later) its Gross Domestic Product (GDP) ranks 163rd of 173 countries for which figures were available. Two-thirds of the population lives below the U.S. poverty line.[46] It has no industry of note, and the only agricultural crop worthy of export is cashews. The formal financial sector in Guinea-Bissau is undeveloped and poorly supervised. And that sector is dwarfed by the size of the underground economy.[47] The UN Office on Drugs and Crime (UNODC) estimates the value of drugs transiting through the country to be $2 billion annually, nominally four times Guinea Bissau's GDP.[48]

Not surprisingly, the country's social and human development indicators are also among the lowest in the world: the UN Development Programme (UNDP) ranked Guinea-Bissau 176th of 187 countries in its 2012 *Human Development Index*.[49] Food security is a major concern at present with approximately 20-30% of rural households considered food insecure.[50]

With so few avenues through which to earn income, competition for office—and the resources that come with it—becomes more critical. Likewise, alternatives to a position in the military and the influence this affords are limited, fueling tensions and competition within the armed forces. For even those in power, managing supporters and patronage networks can be difficult amid such minimal growth. As a result, other "self-financing mechanisms," such as arms and drug trafficking, become increasingly compelling.[51]

This competition for resources and power came to a head in April 2012 when the military leadership felt pressured by former Prime Minister Gomes Junior's bid for the presidency. Several military and political leaders were killed or run off before Army Chief of Staff Indjai arrested Gomes Junior and the interim President to take control of Guinea-Bissau. Most international organizations condemned the coup and demanded a return to democratic rule. However, no one except ECOWAS took punitive steps beyond pulling aid in order to pressure Indjai. ECOWAS muddied the waters by brokering a deal that legitimized the coup and supported Indjai's aims.

All of this turmoil guaranteed Guinea-Bissau a dysfunctional political system that is fragmented in its loyalties, corrupt almost to the core, and disjointed in its approach to solving the nation's overwhelming problems.

Unfortunately, there is no strong national identity that can pull the country toward a solution.

The population of Guinea-Bissau is ethnically diverse and has many distinct languages, customs, and social structures. Nearly 99% of Guineans can be divided into the following three categories:
- The Fula and the Mandinka - who comprise the largest portion of the population and are concentrated in the north and northeast;
- The Balanta and Papel people, who live in the central and southern coastal regions;
- The Manjaco and Mancanha, who occupy the central and northern coastal areas. Most of the remain-

ing 1% are mestiços of mixed Portuguese and black descent.[52]

Aside from interethnic tensions within the military and among civilian elites, there is little indication that rifts have spread to the population as a whole. Interethnic or intercommunal violence is rare. This is to be expected given the broad diversity of ethnic groups within Guinea-Bissau where no single group approaches a majority.[53] There is almost nothing upon which to issue a rallying cry. The social structures are varied, the political system is disjointed, and repeated coups have left a population that is without hope for stability.

Further dividing the country is its geography. The country's main physical features are its meandering rivers and wide estuaries, where it is difficult to distinguish mud, mangrove, and water from solid land. There are six principle rivers traversing a mere 14,000 square miles. Guinea-Bissau also contains a number of coastal islets and an archipelago. The multiple water features throughout the state enhance the divide between peoples and greatly hinders uniting the population into a single nation. It also greatly assists those attempting to circumvent government authority. Guinea-Bissau has neither the manpower nor the assets to effectively govern its coastline, 90 islands, multiple dense forests, and mammoth mangroves.[54]

With no strong national identity, a political system run by warring elites, and a social and physical topography that greatly hinders cohesion within the state, Guinea-Bissau was ripe for renewed exploitation. So at the turn of the century, South American drug lords stepped in. As the Department of States stated in March of 2014,

> Guinea-Bissau is a significant transit hub for drug trafficking from South America to Europe. The country's lack of law enforcement capabilities; demonstrated susceptibility to corruption; porous borders; convenient location between Europe, South America, and neighboring West African transit points; and linguistic connections to Brazil, Portugal, and Cape Verde provide an opportune environment for traffickers. Islands off the coast of Guinea-Bissau are drug trafficking hubs. Guinea-Bissau's political systems remain susceptible to and under the influence of narcotics traffickers; the complicity of government officials at all levels in this criminal activity exacerbates the problem.[55]

It appears that the country's drug market emerged as an acute problem in 2005.[56] At the time, arms smuggling was the preeminent illicit endeavor.[57] President Vieira was amenable to the overtures of drug runners and saw the growing drug trade as a way to improve his, and the country's, economy.[58] He may have even taken a large part in introducing bulk trafficking to the country.[59] As the drug trade expanded, the military, which already had a hand in arms smuggling, became deeply involved. As Vieira and military leaders struggled for power between 2005 and 2008 the huge funds associated with drug trafficking enabled the struggle and kept other parties, with fewer funds, out.[60]

Newspapers and several regional experts have rumored that the 2012 coup, and several accompanying murders, were efforts by South American drug lords, via a few elite military officers, to complete their control of the country.[61] The rapid rise in illegal shipments through Guinea-Bissau in the weeks after the coup appears to corroborate that belief. In April 2013, the U.S. Drug Enforcement Administration (DEA) arrested Admiral Na Tchuto, Chief of the Guinea-Bissau Navy, by posing as Colombian drug traffickers. They also indicted Gen Injai, who remains in Guinea-Bissau overseeing the preparations of new elections. The U.S. Department of State, the U.S. DEA and the UN have labeled Guinea-Bissau as Africa's first narco-state. Its new "colonial" sponsor is a drug cartel out of Colombia, most likely the Fuerzas Armadas Revolucionarias de Colombia rebel militia (FARC).[62] With the U.S. and European Union suspending all relations with Guinea-Bissau, and ECOWAS supporting the leaders of the coup, this illicit neocolonial status is unlikely to change in the near future.[63]

Challenges to dealing with Drug Issues

It seems prudent to look at previous drug wars and identify the challenges to dealing with drug networks before proffering any potential solutions.[64] Considering the context of Guinea-Bissau, there appear to be five issues: the profit paradox, the hydra effect, the authority-resource dilemma, the corrupted sovereign dilemma, and the "It's not my problem" challenge.

> The profit paradox relates to the economic concept of supply and demand. The [global] drug war has been unable to raise the cost of doing business enough to put prices out of range of consumers because the strategy generates a profit paradox: any success in artificially raising prices also inflates profits. These high profits have a paradoxical effect: they provide a steady incentive for drug suppliers to remain in the trade and for new suppliers to enter.[65]

As stated previously, law enforcement must take an unrealistic amount of cocaine out of the market, 75%, before it becomes unprofitable and too risky for drug smugglers to stay in the business.[66]

The hydra effect is closely tied to the profit paradox. Due to the high profitability of running drugs, the low cost of entry into the business, and the high volume of goods that transit the world daily, it is easier for DTOs to shift smuggling routes and move shipment hubs than it is for law enforcement to find and shut them down. Much like the five headed creature of lore, drug kingpins can attack from multiple directions, adapt quickly, and laugh evilly while police lopping off heads barely makes a dent.[67]

Authority and resources issues are especially relevant to Guinea-Bissau. Those who have resources rarely have the necessary authority to tackle the relevant problems, and those with the authorities rarely have the resources. The Guinea-Bissau police are severely under-resourced, and the military is part of the problem.[68] The Economic Community of West African States (ECOWAS), the United Nations (UN), and the International Police (INTERPOL), who have limited financial and manpower resources, are hampered by strict authority boundaries. U.S. Africa Command (AFRICOM), the most resource rich entity in the region, has significant authority limitations. Due to human rights violations in the country, the recent coup, Guinea-Bissau's corrupt military, and the U.S.'s stance on military involvement in law, U.S. governmental laws prevent almost all activities that support Guinea-Bissau's struggling police force or its new fledgling government.[69] The U.S. Department of State, Bureau of International Narcotics and Law Enforcement Affairs (DOS INL) and the Department of Justice's Drug Enforcement Administration (DEA) have the best authorities for foreign counterdrug work, but lack the physical resources to fight a corrupt military and are overstretched financially to deal with the multitude of heads emanating from the global cocaine hydra.

Closely related is the "corrupted sovereign" dilemma. International law favors the sovereignty of a nation state. By treaty and custom, state governments have almost universal authority within their borders. Even when their behaviors violate international law, e.g. supporting drug smuggling, there is little the international body is willing to do. The United Nations installed the United Nations Integrated Peace building Office in Guinea-Bissau (UNIOGBIS) in Guinea-Bissau in 1999, and ECOWAS has had a mission in the country since 2012 (ECOWAS Mission in Guinea-Bissau or ECOMIB). Neither has had much effect due to limited authorities and a reluctance to circumvent the government even when it is obviously corrupt.

One reason sovereigns ignore international law and norms are because they have little negative effect on their nation. "It's not their problem." While the international community may label something "illegal agriculture" or "smuggling," sovereigns may view it as "profitable agriculture" or "lucrative trade" as long as it brings profits to their economy.[70] As African smugglers might put it,

> Trade has always existed; it only becomes smuggling when restrictions are put on trade. It all boils down to two things: smuggling is trade for money, like all trade; and it falls under a set of laws seeking to control the legitimacy of trade. Taxing trade provides money for the powers that be, but it also restricts the power of the traders.[71]

Or as African leaders might put it,

> Extra-state economies are good for business. Most of Africa relies heavily on non-formal business. More than half of the continent's economies run outside of

formal reckoning. But this isn't unusual: half of the economies of Italy, Russia and Peru are extra-state as well.[72]

Since the "extra-state" economy of Guinea-Bissau brings in four times the legal economy, Europe's problem is partly Guinea-Bissau's salvation. Smuggling has been a way of life for centuries, and there is little to no interest in curtailing the drug market until the risks outweigh the benefits.[73]

A Way Ahead for Guinea-Bissau

> Given West Africa's underdevelopment and the global nature of drug trafficking, it is clear that the governments of the subregion cannot respond to this problem — and illicit trafficking in general — without the help and cooperation of regional organizations and the international community.[74]

Guinea-Bissau's way ahead must revolve around reestablishing stable, accountable governance while also increasing the nation's culture of lawfulness. Good governance needs to be established by rewriting the state's constitution, building a feasible economic path forward and neutralizing various spoilers within the current governance system. Simultaneously, the international community must persuade the population to divorce itself from the drug market in a way that does not cause it to concurrently divorce the government in anger. Accomplishing these challenging tasks requires a comprehensive solution[75] and the modification of various U.S. authorities, restrictions and policies.

Guinea-Bissau can never turn the tide until the government rebalances itself away from military rule and provides sufficient checks and balances to begin the fight against corruption. The current system is rife with corruption at every level and since "corruption is an invaluable tool for TCOs"[76] it must be an early target for any effort to aid this small nation. The logical first step is for the newly elected government, just coming out of the first elections since the 2012 coup, to redraft a constitution that pulls power back from the military, establishes appropriate checks and balances within the system, and balances power between the parliament and the president. UNIOGBIS is the ideal organization to support this effort if its charter is expanded beyond rule of law and security sector reform to encompass the wider topic of establishing stable governance.

A restructured system has little hope of survival however, if the economic problems of the country don't improve. The incentive to take money wherever one can find it will obviously be a priority for citizens subject to the economic predicament of Guinea-Bissau. With over two-thirds of the nation below the poverty line and international aid ebbing and flowing as the government convulses every few years, the desire for citizens to do right is repeatedly trumped by the necessity to feed family and tribe. The FARC is playing to this basic survival need to deepen corruption and strengthen its hold on the nation at every turn. The population must see another way forward economically if it is to break free of its new "colonial masters." This should be ECOWAS's aim. As an economic community tied into other international economic communities, ECOWAS in conjunction with the G7+, should make this a top priority in view of the fact that Guinea-Bissau's fate will likely foretell the fate of its neighbors.

There are two spoilers[77] that will challenge these two initial endeavors, the FARC and the Guinea-Bissau military elite. The Guinea-Bissau government, with international support, must neutralize them to accomplish anything worthwhile. Doing this will require four things.

First, the United Nations must invoke Chapter Seven of its charter – the requirement for an international body to restore international peace and security.[78] While many nations are fully aware of the challenges, they are hampered by the "corrupted sovereign" dilemma discussed above. With no effective counterweight to the military elite, an international body must to step in to make any progress. ECOWAS attempted to in 1999 but was obviously ineffective considering where Guinea-Bissau is today. A Chapter Seven invocation would allow ECOWAS, the African Union (AU), the European Union (EU), the North Atlantic Treaty Organization (NATO), INTERPOL, DEA, INL and/or AFRICOM to step in with the right resources, and the right authorities.

Second, the United States must modify its laws and policies to deal with the corrupt sovereign problem. Efforts by DOJ, DOS and DOD to train, enable, and support the police, while keeping the army at bay, require exceptions to various U.S. statues. Congress must grant an exception to policy from the Kennedy and Leahy Amendments to the Foreign Assistance Act[79] (relating to working with nations who have human rights violations), and to existing policy on Foreign Internal Defense support (which requires the host government to invite the U.S. in).

Third, ECOWAS, the AU, the EU and/or the U.S. must find the resources to combat this challenge. While such a small country in Africa would not usually warrant much from any of these organizations, the fact that Guinea-Bissau may be a tipping point for West Africa cannot be ignored. If TCOs are allowed to solidify their control of this "narco-state" then the effects will likely spill over. Guinea-Conakry has already been identified as the next domino getting ready to fall into "narco-state" status. If the international community wants any hope of nipping this problem in the bud it must act now. Nations must look at this problem not as a drug problem, but as a corrupted governance problem likely to reverse several positive trends in African governance.

Fourth, an international coalition must pin down the FARC and the military elite and then neutralize them. This will be challenging, considering the hydra effect. The corrupt elite will be the easier of the two since they are tied to the military, and to the geographic boundaries of Guinea-Bissau. The DEA has already struck once by arresting and prosecuting Admiral Na Tchuto, former Chief of the Guinea-Bissau Navy. With the right authorities and support, U.S. and International Law Enforcement could tamp down the internal TCO leadership until economic and governance efforts began to take effect. Negating FARCs negative role will be much more challenging. The paradox effect, the hydra effect and the resources-authorities dilemma all apply. FARC has the funds and means to ensure that lawlessness is always significantly more profitable that lawfulness. It can shift routes and bases faster than law enforcement can find them. International forces fail if, in the long term, they simply push the FARC to a neighboring country in a never ending game of "Whack-A-Mole". Lastly, the TCOs are well resourced; definitely better than Guinea-Bissau law enforcement units, and most likely better than any international law enforcement brought in to help. The answer is to focus on separating them from government, not on destroying them in total. With appropriate law enforcement assistance from The International Criminal Investigative Training Assistance Program (ICITAP), the Office of Overseas Prosecutorial Development, Assistance, and Training (OPDAT) and those forces dedicated to the West Africa Coast Initiative Transnational Crime Units (WACI TCUs) program, law enforcement units could break the FARC's hold on the Guinea-Bissau government.[80]

> Even in the face of the country's burgeoning drug trade, there have been bright spots in law enforcement. The Judicial Police have made several laudable drug busts, including the arrest of some military figures, though prosecutions have typically foundered in court. Even in the days after the April 2012 coup d'état, the Judicial Police made narcotics-related arrests in Bissau. Despite having little money for fuel or adequate means of transportation, they have developed sources in communities around the country to spot suspicious planes and movement of goods. This progress has continued under several heads of the Judicial Police, suggesting deepening institutional resilience.[81]

"Rule of law is the foundation for economic and political recovery and prosperity..."[82] so ending the spoilers' strangle hold enables long term reforms in government and society.

Obviously, fixing the government and eliminating spoilers are two key top-down approaches. To truly turn Guinea-Bissau around, however, requires a simultaneous bottom up approach. The population must walk away from drug smuggling to finally break the FARC's grip on the nation. Currently the

FARC provide a shadow government to which the population is beholden. International forces must conduct a counter-insurgency effort against the FARC to strip public support away from them and shift it back toward the legitimate government. A good place to start is by publicizing the damage that drugs are doing to Guinea-Bissau families – to make drugs "a local problem" which impacts them negatively vice a foreign problem that only positively affects them by putting money in their pockets. In this endeavor, the TCOs are helping.

> Western African groups have started looking at the region not simply as a transit point, but also as a potential consumer market, leading to an increase in the number of addicts….the UN estimates that about 400 kilograms of heroin were consumed in the first half of 2011 and about 13 metric tonnes of cocaine, with a value of $800m (almost equivalent to Guinea Bissau's GDP) were consumed in the region in 2009. The spread of drug use has a serious impact on society, given the weak public health systems in these countries and the limited number of rehabilitation facilities. [83]

By some estimates eight percent[84] of the world's cocaine users are now from West Africa, with Guinea-Bissau's user problem growing rapidly. The nation's public health infrastructure cannot handle the problem today and the situation grows exponentially worse by the year.

Smuggling has always been an honorable profession in West Africa and trying to change that part of Guinea-Bissau culture is unlikely. But for hundreds of years the products smuggled have not hurt the smugglers themselves. Law Enforcement and government officials can exploit the fact that drugs break that streak.

Historically, the societies of transit countries have never been able to remain immune from the negative impacts of drug trafficking. Inevitably, local consumption of drugs increases, which has cascading negative effects on the social fabric, stability, and security of any transit country. For example, no country in Latin America has suffered as much as Brazil for becoming a key transit country, where payment is often made with drugs; it has become the second largest consumer of cocaine in the world, after the United States. Already, West Africa is proving that it is no exception. [85]

A targeted and robust public information campaign by the Guinea-Bissau government could capitalize on the strong family and tribal bonds of West Africans to make drugs a taboo trade commodity. Messages that promote the honorable tradition of trade (e.g. smuggling) but denounce drugs as toxic to the community may drive smugglers back to guns and cigarettes and away from drugs. This tiny step toward a culture of lawfulness – seeing an illegal product as bad for society – can lead to larger steps down the road. More importantly, however, it may break the FARC's hold long enough to allow legitimate, accountable government to provide for its citizens and turn Guinea-Bissau from "narco-state" into "developing state."

Conclusion

Guinea-Bissau has struggled since the Portuguese drew its borders five centuries ago. Its political structure has thrashed about since it gained independence in 1974 and the government will remain corrupt, disjointed and dysfunctional as long as drug lords control the state's small military elite. There is little to give the country a strong national identity, other than its part in smuggling, and much to keep it divided. As Africa's first narco-state, Guinea-Bissau is in shambles. If the nation hopes to join other developing countries of Africa in their economic and cultural climb, it must shed the burden of drug smuggling. That effort will require finishing governmental structuring work begun in 1974 when Guinea-Bissau became independent, rebalancing power within the society, finding an economic way forward and separating the country's future from TCOs, particularly the FARC. It can be done and if the U.S. truly believes in its *Strategy to Combat Transnational Crime*, and *U.S. Strategy toward Sub-Saharan Africa* then the time to act is now.

Endnotes

1. US Department of State, Bureau for International Narcotics and Law Enforcement Affairs, *International Narcotics Control Reports – Volume I (Drug and Chemical Control)*, (Washington, DC: U.S. Department of State, March 2014): 184 *http://www.state.gov/j/inl/rls/nrcrpt/index.htm* (accessed on 3 Jan 2014).

2. Barak H. Obama, Strategy toward Sub-Saharan Africa, (Washington, DC: The White House, June 2012), 1.

3. Paul Kan, *Drugs and Contemporary Warfare*, (Washington, DC: Potomac Books, 2009), 2.

4. *Ibid.*

5. Eva Bertram, et al., *Drug War Politics: The Price of Denial*, (Berkeley, CA: University of California, 1996) 12.

6. Nigel Inkster, *Drugs, insecurity and failed states: the problems of prohibition*, (Abingdon; New York: Routledge for the International Institute for Strategic Studies, 2012), 16.

7. Barak H. Obama, Strategy to Combat Transnational Organized Crime: Addressing Converging Threats to National Security (Washington, DC: The White House, July 2011), Preamble.

8. *Ibid.*

9. Liana Sun Wyler, *International Drug Control Policy: Background and U.S. Responses* (Washington, DC: U.S. Library of Congress, Congressional Research Service, August 13, 2013), 1.

10. Kan, *Drugs and Contemporary Warfare*, 30.

11. David E. Brown, *The Challenge of Drug Trafficking to Democratic Governance and Human Security in West Africa.* (US Army War College Press: Strategic Studies Institute: Carlisle, PA), 15.

12. Kan, *Drugs and Contemporary Warfare*, 30.

13. Davin O'Regan, *Cocaine and Instability in Africa: Lessons from Latin America and the Caribbean,* (National Defense University, African Center for Strategic Studies: Ft Lesley McNair, Washington DC), 2.

14. James Traub, "Africa's Drug Problem," New York Times Magazine; April 11, 2010, 44.

15. Kwesi Aning & John Pokoo, *Drug Trafficking and Threats to National and Regional Security in West Africa – WACD Background Paper No. 1* (West Africa Commission on Drugs (WACD): Kofi Annan Foundation, 31 January 2013) 3.

16. Brown, *The Challenge of Drug Trafficking to Democratic Governance and Human Security in West Africa*, 3.

17. Aning & Pokoo, *Drug Trafficking and Threats to National and Regional Security in West Africa – WACD Background Paper No. 1, 3.*

18. Brown, *The Challenge of Drug Trafficking to Democratic Governance and Human Security in West Africa*, 22.

19. Max Hoffman & Conor Lane, "Guinea-Bissau and the South Atlantic Cocaine Trade," Center for American Progress,

August 2013, *http://www.americanprogress.org/issues/security/report/2013/08/22/72557/guinea-bissau-and-the-south-atlantic-cocaine-trade/* (accessed 15 Feb 2014).

20. Brown, *The Challenge of Drug Trafficking to Democratic Governance and Human Security in West Africa*, 16.

21. O'Regan, *Cocaine and Instability in Africa: Lessons from Latin America and the Caribbean*, 1.

22. Brown, *The Challenge of Drug Trafficking to Democratic Governance and Human Security in West Africa*, 2.

23. *Ibid*. 16.

24. *Ibid*. 4.

25. *Ibid*. 5.

26. *Ibid*. 1.

27. Obama, Strategy to Combat Transnational Organized Crime, POTUS Letter.

28. *Ibid*. 3.

29. *Ibid*. 5.

30. Obama, Strategy toward Sub-Saharan Africa, 1.

31. *Ibid*.

32. Brown, *The Challenge of Drug Trafficking to Democratic Governance and Human Security in West Africa*, 27.

33. *Ibid*. 40.

34. *Ibid*. iv.

35. *Ibid*. xi.

36. During its colonization period, Guinea-Bissau was named Portuguese Guinea. Upon liberation in 1973 it stripped Portuguese from its name and inserted Bissau (the capital city) in order to differentiate it from its neighbor.

37. Comunidade dos Países de Língua Portuguesa

38. Christopher Clapham, "From Liberation Movement to Government," Brenthurst Foundation Discussion Paper 8/2012 (Johannesburg, SA.: Brenthurst Foundation, November 2012): 5.

39. Davin O'Regan & Peter Thompson, "Advancing Stability and Reconciliation in Guinea-Bissau: Lessons from Africa's First Narco-State," ACSS Special Report # 2, Africa Center for Strategic Studies: 6. *http://africacenter.org/wp-content/uploads/2013/06/ SpecialReport-Guinea-Bissau-JUN2013-EN.pdf* (accessed via on 15 Jan 2014).

40. *Ibid.*

41. "As a whole, then, Guinea-Bissau's military is old, top heavy, over-sized, and suffers from institutional sclerosis. Even after a demobilization campaign following the 1998-1999 civil war reduced the armed forces by roughly half, the military's troop-to-population ratio remains double the West African average. According to a 2008 study (see Table 1), more than half the army is over the age of 40, and 45 percent of all active duty members have more than 20 years of service. Personnel are heavily concentrated in the capital, with 70 percent based in Bissau. There are twice as many senior officers in the armed forces as there are rank and file troops. In other words, the armed forces are less a dynamic and mission-focused institution serving the state than an exclusive club of aging individuals that frequently operates for their personal interests." *Ibid*, 7.

42. *Ibid.* 7.

43. *Ibid.* 9.

44. *Ibid.* 10.

45. Andrexandre Abreu, "Guinea-Bissau Economy," linked from EUROPA WORLD PLUS at *http://www.europaworld.com/entry/gw.ec* (accessed 3 Jan 2014).

46. *The United Nations Integrated Peace-Building Office in Guinea-Bissau Home Page, http://uniogbis.unmissions.org/* (accessed 4 Jan, 2014).

47. US Department of State, *International Narcotics Control Strategy Report (INCSR) – Volume II (Money Laundering)*, Fiscal year 2013 (Washington, DC: U.S. Government Printing Office, 2013), 120. Linked from *http://www.state.gov/j/inl/rls/nrcrpt/index.htm* (accessed on 3 Jan 2014).

48. "UN Police, Justice and Corrections Programming in Guinea-Bissau – a compact study," Stimson: 3, *http://www.stimson.org/images/uploads/research-pdfs/UN_PJC_Programming_in_Guinea-Bissau.pdf* (accessed on 3 Jan 2014).

49. Andrexandre Abreu, "Guinea-Bissau Economy," linked from EUROPA WORLD PLUS at *http://www.europaworld.com/entry/gw.ec* (accessed 3 Jan 2014).

50. *Ibid.*

51. O'Regan & Thompson, "Advancing Stability and Reconciliation in Guinea-Bissau: Lessons from Africa's First Narco-State," 4.

52. UNIOGBIS - United Nations Integrated Peace-Building Office in Guinea-Bissau, "Guinea-Bissau at a Glance," *http://uniogbis.unmissions.org/Default.aspx?tabid=9882&language=en-US* (accessed 3 Jan 2014).

53. O'Regan & Thompson, "Advancing Stability and Reconciliation in Guinea-Bissau: Lessons from Africa's First Narco-State," 23.

54. *The United Nations Integrated Peace-Building Office in Guinea-Bissau Home Page, http://uniogbis.unmissions.org* (accessed 4 Jan, 2014).

55. US Department of State, Bureau for International Narcotics and Law Enforcement Affairs, *International Narcotics Control Reports – Volume I (Drug and Chemical Control)*, (Washington, DC: U.S. Department of State, March 2014): 120 *http://www.state.gov/j/inl/rls/nrcrpt/index.htm* (accessed on 3 Jan 2014).

56. *The United Nations Integrated Peace-Building Office in Guinea-Bissau Home Page, http://uniogbis.unmissions.org* (accessed 4 Jan, 2014).

57. O'Regan & Thompson, "Advancing Stability and Reconciliation in Guinea-Bissau: Lessons from Africa's First Narco-State," 17.

58. *Ibid.* 31.

59. *Ibid.*

60. *Ibid*

61. Max Hoffman & Conor Lane, "Guinea-Bissau and the South Atlantic Cocaine Trade," Center for American Progress, August 2013, *http://www.americanprogress.org/issues/security/report/2013/08/22/72557/guinea-bissau-and-the-south-atlantic-cocaine-trade/* (accessed 15 Feb 2014).

62. Brown, *The Challenge of Drug Trafficking to Democratic Governance and Human Security in West Africa*, 21.

63. Max Hoffman & Conor Lane, "Guinea-Bissau and the South Atlantic Cocaine Trade," Center for American Progress, August 2013, *http://www.americanprogress.org/issues/security/report/2013/08/22/72557/guinea-bissau-and-the-south-atlantic-cocaine-trade/* (accessed 15 Feb 2014).

64. Eva Bertram identifies three flaws in the war on drugs in her book *Drug War Politics: the Price of Denial*. This paper discusses two: The Profit Paradox and the Hydra Effect.

65. Bertram, et al., *Drug War Politics: The Price of Denial*, 13.

66. Kan, *Drugs and Contemporary Warfare*, 80.

67. "Alexander Schmidt, head of the U.N. drug office in West Africa, says he was struck by the astonishing nimbleness of the traffickers, who seem to pick up and discard routes and countries spontaneously." James Traub, "Africa's Drug Problem," New York Times Magazine; April 11, 2010, 44.

68. Helmoed Heitman, *Optimizing Africa's Security Force Structures*, (National Defense University, African Center for Strategic Studies: Ft Lesley McNair, Washington DC), 2.

69. "US policy as well as well as the 1978 "Kennedy Amendment" to the FAA (Title 22, USC, Section 2304[a] [2]) prevents US cooperation with and SA funding to a government of any country that engages in a consistent pattern of gross violations of internationally recognized human rights." U.S. Department of Defense, Foreign Internal Defense, Joint Publication 3-22, pg VI-9.
"The "Leahy Amendment" contains additional constraints on government funding of SFA/FID missions. The law, first enacted in the 1997 Foreign Operations Appropriations Act (the annual DOS appropriations act), prohibits the USG from providing funds to the security forces of a foreign country if DOS has credible evidence that the foreign country or its agents have committed gross violations of human rights, unless the Secretary of State determines and reports that the government of such country is taking effective measures to bring the responsible members of the security forces to justice." U.S. Department of Defense, Foreign Internal Defense, Joint Publication 3-22, pg A-7.
"Absent direction from SecDef, DOD forces engaged in CD activities are prohibited from engaging in direct law enforcement activity. They may not directly participate in an arrest, search, seizure, or other similar activity. DOD personnel are not authorized to accompany HN forces on actual CD field operations or participate in any activities where hostilities are likely to occur." U.S. Department of Defense, Foreign Internal Defense, Joint Publication 3-22, pg VI-6.

70. O'Regan, *Cocaine and Instability in Africa: Lessons from Latin America and the Caribbean*, 2.

71. Carolyn Nordstrom, *Global Outlaws*, (Berkeley, CA: University of California Press, 2007), 161.

72. *Ibid*, 109.

73. O'Regan, *Cocaine and Instability in Africa: Lessons from Latin America and the Caribbean*, 2.

74. Brown, *The Challenge of Drug Trafficking to Democratic Governance and Human Security in West Africa*, 43.

75. US Institute for Peace and U.S. Army Peacekeeping and Stability Operations Institute, Guiding Principles for Stabilization and Reconstruction, (Washington DC: Endowment of the United States Institute for Peace, 2009), 1-2.

76. Kelly Greenhill, "Kleptocratic Interdependence" in Robert Rotberg ed., *Corruption, Global Security and World Order*, Washington, DC: Brookings Institution, 2009, 99.

77. "Spoilers are individuals or parties who believe that the peace process threatens their power and interests and will therefore work to undermine it." US Institute for Peace and U.S. Army Peacekeeping and Stability Operations Institute, Guiding Principles for Stabilization and Reconstruction, (Washington DC: Endowment of the United States Institute for Peace, 2009), 3-20.

78. United Nations Homepage, *http://www.un.org/en/documents/charter/chapter7.shtml* (accessed on 5 Jan 2014).

79. See endnote 68.

80. "Five major international agreements underpin and provide near global scope to our efforts to combat TOC and corruption: the United Nations Convention against Transnational Organized Crime (UNTOC), its three supplementary protocols against trafficking in persons, migrant smuggling, and illicit trafficking in firearms, and the United Nations Convention against Corruption (UNCAC). The United States strongly supports the framework provided by these instruments, especially with regard to prosecuting and investigating transnational crime and corruption, engaging in mutual legal assistance, and supplementing bilateral extradition treaties." Barak H. Obama, Strategy to Combat Transnational Organized Crime: Addressing Converging Threats

to National Security (Washington, DC: The White House, July 2011), 5.

81. O'Regan & Thompson, "Advancing Stability and Reconciliation in Guinea-Bissau: Lessons from Africa's First Narco-State," 15.

82. US Institute for Peace and U.S. Army Peacekeeping and Stability Operations Institute, Guiding Principles for Stabilization and Reconstruction, (Washington DC: Endowment of the United States Institute for Peace, 2009), 7-75.

83. Inkster, *Drugs, insecurity and failed states: the problems of prohibition*, 107.

84. Brown, *The Challenge of Drug Trafficking to Democratic Governance and Human Security in West Africa*, 37.

85. *Ibid.*

U.S. ARMY WAR COLLEGE

Major General William E. Rapp
Commandant

*****

PEACEKEEPING & STABILITY OPERATIONS INSTITUTE

Director
Colonel Daniel A. Pinnell

Assistant Director
Professor William J. Flavin

Author
Colonel Stephen K. Van Riper

Publications Coordinator
Mr. R. Christopher Browne

*****

Composition
Mrs. Jennifer E. Nevil

www.ingramcontent.com/pod-product-compliance
Lightning Source LLC
Chambersburg PA
CBHW071146280526
45787CB00003B/1427